Cash, Credit Cards, or Checks

A Book About Payment Methods

written by Nancy Loewen * illustrated by Brad Fitzpatrick

Thanks to our advisers for their expertise, research, and advice:

Dr. Joseph Santos
Associate Professor of Economics, Department of Economics
South Dakota State University

Susan Kesselring, M.A., Literacy Educator
Rosemount-Apple Valley-Eagan (Minnesota) School District

PICTURE WINDOW BOOKS
Minneapolis, Minnesota

Managing Editor: Catherine Neitge
Creative Director: Terri Foley
Art Director: Keith Griffin
Editors: Patricia Stockland, Christianne Jones
Designer: Nathan Gassman
Page production: Picture Window Books
The illustrations in this book were
prepared digitally.

Picture Window Books
5115 Excelsior Boulevard
Suite 232
Minneapolis, MN 55416
877-845-8392
www.picturewindowbooks.com

**Library of Congress
Cataloging-in-Publication Data**
Loewen, Nancy, 1964-
Cash, credit cards, or checks : a book about
payment methods / written by Nancy
Loewen ; illustrated by Brad Fitzpatrick.
p. cm. — (Money matters)
Includes bibliographical references
and index.
ISBN 1-4048-0951-1 (hardcover)
1. Money—Juvenile literature. 2. Checks—
Juvenile literature. 3. Credit cards—Juvenile
literature. 4. Debit cards—Juvenile
literature. I. Fitzpatrick, Brad. II. Title.
III. Money matters (Minneapolis, Minn.)

HG221.5.L53 2005
332.4—dc22   2004018428

"All right," Dad said. "It's time to go back-to-school shopping. Do you both have your school supply lists?"

"YES!" Amy and Kyle yelled.

Dad made sure he had his wallet and checkbook. "Let's hit the road!" he said.

At Merry-Mart, Kyle and Amy began putting supplies into the cart.

Dad said, "It looks like I'm going to have to write a pretty big check."

"Just write a check for a million dollars. That should cover all of our supplies," said Kyle.

"It doesn't quite work that way," laughed Dad.

You can only write a check for as much money as you have in your bank account.

5

At the register, Dad took out his checkbook. He wrote the date, the store's name, and the total amount in numbers and in words. Dad also wrote down the date, check number, and amount in a little notebook.

"What's that notebook for?" asked Kyle.

A check tells the bank to take that amount of money out of your account and pay it to the person or store on the check.

"This is a register. It helps me keep track of how much money I have in my checking account," Dad answered.

Next they went to the mall.
Amy looked for backpacks.
She liked a fancy orange one.
She also liked a
purple one
with wheels,
but it cost
$10 more.

"Just get the
orange one.
It's cheaper,"
Kyle said.

"It is cheaper. But I'm buying the one with wheels," she said. "My books get heavier every year! Besides, I put enough money in my checking account for a good backpack this year."

Plan how you will pay for the things you need before you buy them. Price isn't the only thing to think about. You want to make quality purchases that you will be happy with.

"When did you get a credit card?" Kyle asked Amy, as she pulled out a plastic card.

"It's not a credit card. It's a debit card," Amy answered. "The debit card goes with my checking account, but it's faster than writing a check. It works the same way, though. The bank takes money out of my account and pays the store."

When a debit card is used, a record of the purchase will appear on a monthly statement.

The Robertsons' next stop was a big department store. Amy tried on lots of jeans. She came out of the dressing room holding three pairs.

"I really like the designer jeans," she said, "but I can get both of these, plus a belt, for the same money. So that's what I'm going to do."

"I saw a sign that said if you buy any pair of shoes, you get the second pair for half price. Can I get two pairs, Dad?" Kyle asked.

"Okay," Dad said. "Your shoes do wear out in a hurry. You could use another pair."

The clerk scanned Amy's purchases. This time, Dad paid with his credit card. The clerk handed him a receipt to sign and made sure his signature matched the back of the card. The clerk kept that receipt and gave Dad a different one.

TOTAL $37.72

BURT

Many people use credit cards because they are safer than cash. If you lose your credit card, you can cancel it so people can't use it. If you lose cash, anyone can spend it.

14

"Does that take money out of an account, too?" asked Kyle.

"No," Dad answered. "This is an easy way of borrowing money. The credit card company pays the store, and then I pay the credit card company."

On the way to the food court, the Robertsons stopped at a computer store.

Kyle had been saving his allowance for the latest version of Frenzied Frogs Xtreme. The price was still more money than Kyle had.

Some stores have credit cards that can only be used there. These stores give extra discounts, or savings, for using their card.

"I'll put it on my Great Buy card," Dad suggested. "Then you can pay me back. If we use the store's card, we save $10. Then you'll have enough for the game."

"Thanks a bunch!" Kyle said.

Dad was low on cash, so he headed for the nearest ATM. He used his debit card to make a withdrawal.

"What does ATM stand for?" Kyle asked.

"Automatic teller machine. It's like a human teller at a bank," Amy answered.

"Kind of like a robot!" said Kyle. "Cool!"

Amy continued, "If you have money in your account, you can get cash. You can also make deposits and move money between accounts. The machine reads your account number from the magnetic strip on your card. Then you enter your PIN. That's your own secret code."

PIN stands for personal identification number.

"And now," said Dad, "this is the moment I've been waiting for all day. I'm going to sit down and take a break. Here's some cash. Please go get us some ice cream."

And don't forget to bring
me the change!"

Credit Card Diagram

Account Number ----→ **0000 0000 0000 0000**
0000

GOOD THRU 07/26

Cardholder's Name ---→ **SMARTY T. PIG**

Card Expiration Date

Barn Bank International

Cardholder's Signature --→ *Smarty the Pig*

0000000000000000 000

Magnetic Strip
tells machine account information

Fun Facts

- Many people use computer programs to keep track of their money and make a budget.

- Shoppers should keep their receipts in case they need to make a return. This tells the store when and where you bought the item and how much you paid for it.

- ATMs are connected to large computer networks between banks.

- Flyers are printed pages that list a store's sales. These ads are often put in newspapers. In large cities, half of the Sunday paper is advertising.

- Sometimes you are charged a small fee for using the ATM if your bank does not own the machine.

- At the end of the month, your credit card company sends a bill of all your purchases. If you don't pay the whole bill, you have to pay extra money called interest.

Glossary

bank—an organization that provides financial services

budget—a plan for spending money

deposit—to add money to an account

interest—the cost of borrowing money

statement—a list of all the money events that happened in an account over a certain period of time (usually a month)

withdrawal—to take money out of an account

TO LEARN MORE

At the Library

Hall, Margaret. *Credit Cards and Checks*. Chicago: Heinemann Library, 2000.

Rosinsky, Natalie. *Spending Money*. Minneapolis: Compass Point Books, 2004.

Stone, L. *Paying by Credit*. Vero Beach, Fla.: Rourke Publishing, 2003.

On the Web

FactHound offers a safe, fun way to find Web sites related to this book. All of the sites on FactHound have been researched by our staff.
www.facthound.com

1. Visit the FactHound home page.

2. Enter a search word related to this book, or type in this special code: 1404809511

3. Click on the fetch it button.

Your trusty FactHound will fetch the best sites for you!

Look for all of the books in this series:

- Cash, Credit Cards, or Checks: A Book About Payment Methods

- Lemons and Lemonade: A Book About Supply and Demand

- Save, Spend, or Donate? A Book About Managing Money

- Ups and Downs: A Book About the Stock Market